THE VIZ BOOK OF CRAP JOKES

A COMPILATION OF PISS-POOR QUALITY SECOND HAND, THIRD RATE JOKES FROM THE PAGES OF VIZ MAGAZINE

Cobbled together hurriedly by Chris Donald
Simon Thorp, Graham Dury & Simon Donald

*With special thanks to Roger Radio
Jim Biz, Brent Russell, Tony Harding
and everyone else who contributed to this book*

HOW TO ENJOY YOUR NEW BOOK OF JOKES

Congratulations. You are now the owner of possibly the world's greatest collection of poor quality jokes. If read correctly this book will probably give you several minutes of pleasure. Here are a few tips to help you get the most from your book of crap jokes.

1 Make sure you are comfortable, relaxed and in a pleasant frame of mind before attempting to read any jokes. (Perhaps you'd like to make yourself a cup of tea or coffee if you prefer, and settle back with a biscuit or scone in your favourite armchair). Try to wear loose and comfortable clothing whenever possible. Take the phone off the hook, and remove the batteries from your door bell.

2 Pace yourself properly. Don't try to read too many jokes in one go. Read two or three to begin with, then give yourself a break. Stretch your legs, take the dog for a walk. On your return you will feel refreshed and ready to continue. Under no circumstances should you attempt to read the entire book in one session.

3 If you feel that you have not enjoyed a particular joke, don't worry, this is perfectly normal. It happens to everybody. Simply pass the joke over and return to it later when you are feeling more at ease and confident about the joke. It it still fails to amuse you, chat about it with a more intelligent friend or someone who wears glasses. If you fail to enjoy a large proportion of the jokes in this book, mention it to your local G.P. – he may be able to help.

The joke shown opposite has been broken down into its constituent parts by Dr. Alistair Morris, Professor of Jokes at Loughborough University. Investing ten or twenty minutes in a careful study of this sample joke will pay great dividends in enhancing your enjoyment of the subsequent pages.

FEED LINE

Always read this first – it conveys vital information necessary to understand the joke. In certain jokes it may be absent, in which case all the necessary information will be contained in the illustration itself. (These jokes are known as Ham Gags). The feed line itself **IS NOT FUNNY**, laugh at this and you have completely misunderstood the joke.

PUNCH LINE

This is the **FUNNY** line and should be read only when you are confident that you have gained all the requisite comedy information from the feed line (qv) and/or illustration. Directly upon reading the punch line the joke should become apparent and laughter should ensue. If after ten seconds or so you have failed to laugh, you have failed to understand the joke and you should start to read it again from the beginning.

STRAIGHT MAN

In layman's terms it is the job of the straight man to 'tee up' the joke in as humourless a manner as possible, thus enabling the funny man (qv) to deliver the punch line (qv). Where the straight man is inactive, i.e. in a ham gag (qv), he is known as the stooge.

FUNNY MAN

It is the funny man's job to 'carry' the gag, thus 'putting it across' to the reader. His delivery of the punch line is the keystone upon which the entire joke is hinged, and upon which it will either stand or fall. The impact of the punch line is often accentuated by the physical appearance of the funny man. He may wear a funny hat, have checked trousers, big ears or some other visibly amusing characteristic. In this case the artist has elected to draw him badly and with a prominent nose in order to make it funnier.

COMEDY PROPS

Also known as 'joke furniture', these are specific objects or items featured in the illustration and vital to the mechanics of the joke. These are the axels upon which the wheel of comedy spins.

INDICATION LABELS

These are included in order to convey bulk information vital to the joke, and often to firmly locate the scenario. They many take the form of folded desk signs, shop signs, fixed wall signs or large oblong signs suspended from nowhere by two pieces of string.

6

11

13

14

18

19

Famous People On The Toilet

No. 72   Neville Chamberlain

THE GREAT TRAIN ROBBERY

WELL, IT WAS HERE A MINUTE AGO...

ROGER RADIO 87

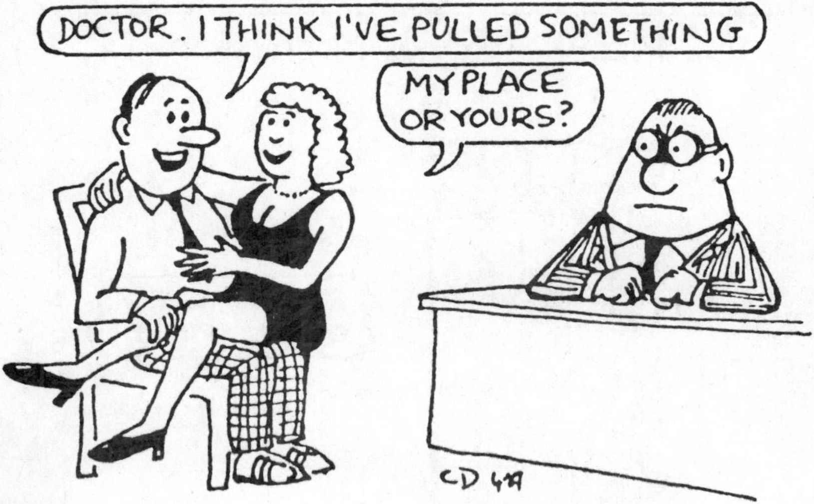
DOCTOR. I THINK I'VE PULLED SOMETHING
MY PLACE OR YOURS?
CD 4A

Famous People On The Toilet

No. 97 Magnus Magnusson

29

30

Famous People On The Toilet

No. 364 Rolf Harris

FISH JOKE

CD 19.9.90.

39

40

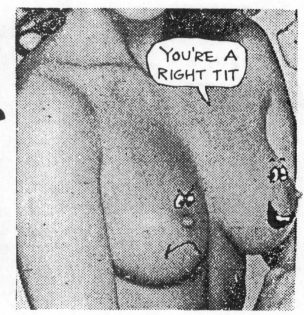

43

44

47

48

A man treating his fence with creosote

51

52

'REF, CAN YOU CLEAN THE WHITE BALL— I THINK THERE'S A HARE ON IT!'

53

LAZY
SOD

58

60

61

THE DAY OF THE TRIFFIDS

SPIDER JOKE

Victor Mature

73

74

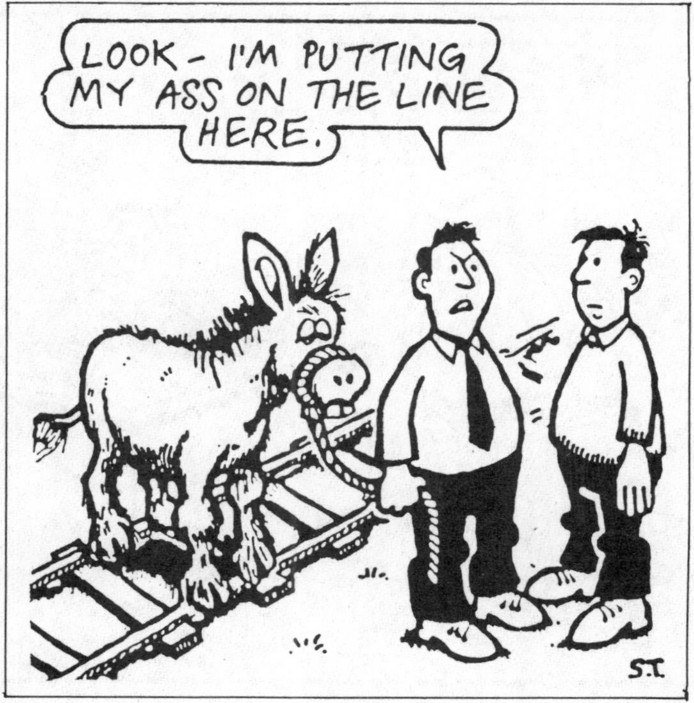
LOOK - I'M PUTTING MY ASS ON THE LINE HERE.
S.T.

Tailors Shop Joke

83

Tailors Shop Joke

85

87

89

JOKE INDEX

Animal and Plant Jokes

Ass on the line 78
Hare on the ball 53
It's a jungle 71
Lazy sod 57
Snake charmer 16
Spiders 66
Triffids 64
Whales 70

Drinks Jokes

Beer talking 59
See your drinks off 44

Doctor Jokes

Animal inside 72
Ate something 1
Ate something II 2
Bad haddock 28
Bad signs 58
Boyle on bottom 51
Caught something 54
Coming down 85
Critical condition 15
Diarrhoea (clearing up) 30
Diarrhoea (case of) 77
Feeling faint 21
Feeling flushed 74
Feeling fragile 48
Give it to me 69
Hair falling out 43
It's my heart 65
Little horse 62
Little saw 90
Mind playing tricks 83
Neck complaint 11
Over the hill 46
Pain in chest 36
Pain in dressing table 37
Picked up bug 55
Pulled something 25
Putting weight on 34
Round the bend 75
Run down 40
Shadow 80
Stone mason's chisel 91
Unattractive wife 19
Upset stomach 9
Wife swapping 18
Wrong joke 86

Fish Jokes

Believe in cod 42
What's a nice plaice 14
Your plaice or mine 32

Miscellaneous Jokes

Enemy planes 87
Got your elf 45
Mark of Zorro 38
Pompeii 82
Right tit 41
Spoil myself 47
Train robbery 24
Treating a fence 50
Victor Mature 68